J. T. Surenne

The Dance Music of Scotland

A Collection of All the Best Reels and Strathspeys Both of the Highlands...

J. T. Surenne

The Dance Music of Scotland
A Collection of All the Best Reels and Strathspeys Both of the Highlands...

ISBN/EAN: 9783744793438

Printed in Europe, USA, Canada, Australia, Japan

Cover: Foto ©Thomas Meinert / pixelio.de

More available books at **www.hansebooks.com**

THE

DANCE MUSIC OF SCOTLAND

A COLLECTION OF ALL THE BEST

REELS AND STRATHSPEYS

BOTH OF THE HIGHLANDS AND LOWLANDS

FOR THE PIANOFORTE

ARRANGED AND EDITED

BY

J. T. SURENNE.

SIXTH EDITION.

EDINBURGH:

WOOD AND CO., 49 GEORGE STREET.

INTRODUCTION.

This Collection contains two hundred and forty-five of the best Reels and Strathspeys of the Highlands and the Lowlands of Scotland, arranged expressly for the Pianoforte. The correct notation of the tunes has been carefully attended to, and their harmonic arrangement is new. The tunes are distributed into sets of three, as they are generally danced; that is to say, Reel, Strathspey, Reel. The proper *tempo* of each tune is indicated according to Maelzel's Metronome. In some rare instances the key is changed in order to facilitate Pianoforte performance; and in many of the tunes the proper fingering of certain passages is marked. Several Dance-tunes are not included in this Collection, because they have become intimately associated with Songs by Burns and other Scottish Poets. These tunes, however, will be found in " Wood's Songs of Scotland," and also in " Wood's Melodies of Scotland without Words." To increase the usefulness and popularity of this Volume, the writer of the Introduction has given, from a scarce work, a complete description of all the true Highland Steps of the Reel and the Strathspey, with their original Gaelic names. By means of that description, and of the numerous tunes given in this Collection, the dancing of Reels and Strathspeys may be learned and practised by the families of Scottish settlers in the remotest parts of the globe.

As this volume is devoted to the National Dance Music of Scotland, viz., Reels and Strathspeys, we think it unnecessary to say much about other Dance Music which was brought hither from France or England. In the oldest Scottish Collections of manuscript music[1] we find Allemandes, Branles, Courantes, Gaillardes, Gavottes, Voltes[2]—dances derived by us from France, although not all of them of French origin—and along with these some Scottish dance-tunes and a few English ones. These MSS. show the preponderance of foreign dances and dance-tunes in Scotland at that time, and long before then at the Scottish Court, when Reels and Strathspeys were as yet only among future possibilities of fashion.[3]

Fifty years ago, the fashionable Dances taught in Edinburgh and other large towns in Scotland, were Minuets, Cotillons, Reels and Strathspeys, and Country-Dances. Now, with the exception of the Reels and Strathspeys, all these Dances have disappeared and made way for the Waltz, the Polka, &c., &c.; which last will, in turn, yield their places to some other saltatory novelties. But the Reels and Strathspeys have held their ground, manfully and womanfully, in both Scotland and England to this day; and we are not sure that they have not, of late years, found their way even to France, that soil of all soils the most bedanced by merry lads and lasses. The high popularity of the Reel and the Strathspey, all over Great Britain, induces us to dwell more particularly and minutely upon these Dances, which are really the only National Dances of Scotland; all our other Dances of ancient or modern times having been derived by us from France or from England.

In the Collection of Highland Airs, published in 1781 by the Rev. Patrick M'Donald,[4] he mentions (in the Preface) some particulars regarding the manner in which these airs are sung or played by the natives. " The slow plaintive

---

[1] The Straloch, and Skene, and Rowallan, and Leyden MSS. See List appended to this volume.
[2] The Volte was anciently a common dance in Provence, and was originally the Italian Volta. It somewhat resembled the Modern Waltz. For a description of " La Volta," and of various other dances of the sixteenth century, see Sir John Davies' poem on Dancing, written about 1590. Byron's bitter attack upon the Waltz is well known.
[3] It will be seen afterwards that these Scottish Dances were much in vogue fifty years ago, and were taught at the Court of England Her Majesty Queen Victoria, on first visiting the Highlands, was much struck with these dances, and has since patronized them.
[4] See No. 24 of List given in this volume.

tunes are sung by the natives in a wild, artless, and irregular manner. Chiefly occupied with the sentiment and expression of the music, they dwell upon the long and pathetic notes, while they hurry over the inferior and connecting notes in such a manner as to render it exceedingly difficult for a hearer to trace the measure of them. They themselves, while singing them, seem to have little or no impression of measure." (P. 2.) As his work is now rare, we subjoin what he says regarding the Harp Music of the Highlands. "The Airs above-mentioned, and others of similar structure, are valuable, as probably being the most genuine remains of the ancient Harp Music of the Highlands. This was once the favourite music in the Highlands of Scotland, as it has long continued to be in Ireland. The fate, however, which it has experienced in the two countries, has been very different. In Ireland the harpers, the original composers and the chief depositaries of that music, have, till lately, been uniformly cherished and supported by the nobility and gentry. They endeavoured to outdo one another in playing the airs that were most esteemed, with correctness, and with their proper expression. Such of them as were men of abilities, attempted to adorn them with graces and variations, or to produce what were called good sets of them. These were communicated to their successors, and by them transmitted with additions.[1] By this means the pieces were preserved, and so long as they continued in the hands of the native harpers, we may suppose that they were gradually improved, as whatever graces and variations they added to them, were consistent with, and tending to heighten and display the genuine spirit and expression of the music. The taste for that style of performance seems now, however, to be declining. The native harpers are not much encouraged. A number of their airs have come into the hands of foreign musicians, who have attempted to fashion them according to the model of the modern music; and these new sets are considered in the country as capital improvements. *The Lady in the Desart*, as played by an old harper, and as played according to the sets now in fashion, can hardly be known to be the same tune. It is now abundantly regular in its structure; but its native character and expression, its wildness and melancholy, are gone. The variations are such as might have been composed at this day in Italy or Germany. In the Highlands of Scotland, again, the harp has long ceased to be the favourite instrument; and, for upwards of a century, has been seldom heard. The encouragement of the people has been transferred to the bagpipe, an instrument more congenial to the martial spirit of the country. In consequence of this, many of the pieces that had been originally composed, and had been chiefly performed or accompanied by the harpers, are irrecoverably lost; and those which have been preserved by tradition, may naturally be supposed to have been gradually degenerating."—P. 3.

"A considerable number of the airs contained in this first division[2] are what the country people call *Luinigs*, and are sung when a number of persons are assembled, either at work or for recreation. They are generally short; their measure is regular, and the cadences are distinctly marked. Many of them are chorus songs. Particular parts of the tune are allotted to the principal singer, who expresses the significant words; the other parts are sung in chorus by the whole company present.[3] These pieces being simple and airy, are easily remembered, and have probably been accurately preserved."

In the Dissertation[4] prefixed to the same Collection, Mr. Young tells us that the people of St. Kilda, at the close of the fishing season, when they have laid up their winter store, meet together rejoicingly in the store-house, and there sing and dance to one of their best reel tunes, (p. 9.) He mentions also the *luinigs* and the *iorrums*, or boat-songs of the men, to which they keep time with their oars when rowing, (p. 10.) "The St. Kildians too are very fond of music. Being great lovers of dancing, they have a number of reels, which are either sung or played on the Jew's harp, or trump, their only musical instrument. One or two of these sound uncommonly wild, even to one that can relish a rough Highland Reel. Some of the notes appear to be borrowed from the cries of the sea-fowl which visit them at certain seasons of the year, and are considered as their benefactors. Their elegiac music is in a better strain, pathetic and melancholy, but exceedingly simple. Like the other peculiarities of the Highlanders, the custom of singing these songs *regularly* at work is declining apace, especially in the eastern countries and the districts which have much intercourse with the Lowlanders. Yet, less than a century ago, it was practised by their forefathers. However wild and artless some of the *luinigs* may be, and however ill others of them are sung by the common people, yet a number of beautiful original ones may still be collected in the Highlands. The greater part of them appear to be adapted to the harp, an instrument which was once in high estimation there."—(*Ibid.*, p. 11.) Giraldus Cambrensis,[5] who visited

---

[1] This is quite opposed to Bunting's strange assertion, that the oldest Irish airs were preserved by tradition unchanged, through a series of generations of harpers.

[2] Chiefly from Ross-shire and Sutherlandshire.

[3] These songs appear to have some analogy to those of the Faröe Isles mentioned at p. 8 of Introduction to "Wood's Vocal Melodies of Scotland without Words." Mr. Robert Jamieson, the editor of the "Northern Antiquities," intended to procure from Orkney the popular melody or chant to which the Norse Song of "The Weird Sisters," which the Orcadians call "The Enchantresses," was commonly sung; all traces of it having long since been lost in Scandinavia. We know not whether he did procure that melody.

[4] Written by the Rev. Walter Young, afterwards D.D. He became Minister of Erskine in Renfrewshire in 1772, and died at an advanced age on 6th August 1814.

[5] Gir. Cambr. Topog. Hib., lib. ii. c. ii.

Ireland about the year 1185, gives a curious account of the skill of Irish harpers, and mentions that the Scots and Welsh learned their art from the Irish, and that, in the opinion of many, the Scots far excelled the Irish. John Major[1] tells that in the fifteenth century the Irish and the Scottish Highlanders were the most eminent harpers then known. Mr. Young says,—" But beyond all memory or tradition, the bagpipe has been the favourite instrument of that people, (the Highlanders.) The large bagpipe is their instrument for war, for marriage or funeral processions, and for other great occasions. They have also a smaller kind upon which dancing-tunes are played. In their hours of merriment and relaxation, young people of both sexes danced with great alacrity to a species of wild airy tunes, the nature of which is universally known."—*Ibid.*, p. 12. Mr. Young states, that " that peculiar species of martial music, the *pibroch* or *cruineachadh*, was sometimes sung, accompanied with words, but more frequently performed on the bagpipe." " The contrast between the pipe and the harp tunes is so striking, that one could hardly imagine them to be the music of the same people. Indeed, none of the *luinigs* is adapted to the bagpipe."[2]—*Ibid.*, p. 13.

Besides the modern Irish Bagpipe, which has the softest sound of all Bagpipes, the Irish claim for themselves an ancient Bagpipe, large and loud, of the same kind as our Scottish Highland one. Bunting states that the large Bagpipe was the proper military musical instrument of the Irish in the fifteenth century, and Mr. Petrie, the Irish antiquary, informs us that the bagpipe is often mentioned in Irish poems, varying in date between the tenth and sixth centuries.

For many years the Violin has taken place of the Bagpipe in most parts of Scotland, for playing of Reels, Strathspeys, and other Highland dance-tunes. Captain Simon Fraser, in his Collection of Highland Airs, mentions that Grant of Sheugly, who was a poet and a player on the violin, bagpipe, and harp, gave the preference to the violin for Dance Music.[3] Neil Gow and his sons greatly promoted the use of the violin for the Dance Music of Scotland.

Francis Peacock, who published the Collection of Scottish Airs cited in No. 20 of the List given in this volume, was an eminent Dancing-Master in Aberdeen, and died there in June 1807, aged 84, leaving a considerable bequest of money to the charitable institutions of that town. In 1805, he published " Sketches relative to the History[4] and Theory, but more especially to the Practice of Dancing," &c., &c., 1 vol. 8vo, pp. 224. Aberdeen, Angus and Son : London, Longman and Co. : Edinburgh, Archibald Constable. As that volume contains some curious information regarding the Dance Music and Dances of Scotland at that time, and is now very rare, we quote the following passages from it, leaving our readers to make due allowances for the author's professional enthusiasm in some particulars. It is worth while to record *what* these National Scottish Dances really were half a century ago.[5]

" Sketch V. Observations on the Scotch Reel, with a description of the fundamental steps made use of in that Dance, and their appropriate Gaelic names.—The fondness the Highlanders have for this Quartett, or Trio, (for it is either one or the other,) is unbounded ; and so is their ambition to excel in it. This pleasing propensity, one would think, was born with them, from the early indications we sometimes see their children shew for this exercise. I have seen children of theirs, at five or six years of age, attempt, nay, even execute some of their steps so well as almost to surpass belief. I once had the pleasure of seeing, in a remote part of the country, a Reel danced by a herd boy and two young girls, who surprised me much, especially the boy, who appeared to be about twelve years of age. He had a variety of well-chosen steps, and executed them with so much justness and ease, as if he meant to set criticism at defiance. Circumstances like these plainly evince that those qualities must either be inherent in the Highlanders, or that they must have an uncommon aptitude for imitation. Our Colleges draw hither,[6] every year, a number of students from the Western Isles, as well as from the Highlands, and the greater part of them excel in this dance; some of them indeed in so superior a degree, that I myself have thought them worthy of imitation. I mention these circumstances with no other view but as an introduction to what I am about to offer in relation to the steps most used in the Scotch Reels. To those who already know them, all I mean to say will be useless ; but to others who have been wanting in opportunities of seeing this dance well performed, a description of the steps best adapted to those lively tunes, which have obtained the name of the dance to which they gave birth, may not, upon the whole, be unacceptable ; especially as it is no uncommon thing at Edinburgh to see men of our profession, who come there with no other view but to acquire a knowledge of the proper steps made use of in that dance. It is not long since two of them (father[7] and son) came from London to Edinburgh for no other purpose ; and, as they had their own carriage, it may be presumed they must have been men of some reputation in their profession. They made application to the most fashionable teacher of dancing in that place,[8] but

[1] De Gest. Scot., lib. vi.

[2] In the note on the Bagpipe which we furnished to Mr. Dauney for his Dissertation, p. 125, we show that, in old writers, the word " chorus" often meant a " bagpipe."

[3] See note on No. 3 of Captain Fraser's Collection, and also note at page 51 of the third volume of " Wood's Songs of Scotland."

[4] Any one who wishes to involve himself in the inextricable mazes of discussion regarding the dances of the Ancients, may find ample materials for his confusion in the writings of learned commentators upon the classics.

[5] We are indebted to Mr. James Davie, the well-known Teacher of Music in Aberdeen, for a perusal of this rare volume.   [6] To Aberdeen.

[7] We are informed that these two Dancing-Masters were, most probably, Mr. Jenkins and his son. Jenkins was a native of Inver, near Dunkeld—went to London to teach dancing—became Court Dancing-Master, and made a large fortune.

[8] This must have been either Strange, or Richard Barnard, the owner of " Barnard's Rooms," Thistle Street, or his successor Andrew Laurie

as he was then too busy preparing for a ball to be of much use to them himself, he recommended them to my partner, who happened to be then at Edinburgh. On his return, he told me that (their time as well as his own being limited) he attended them two or three times a day during their stay there. I mention this circumstance as a proof of what importance they thought a right knowledge of the dance might be to them on their return to London. Before I attempt to describe the principal steps made use of in Scotch Reels, it may be proper first to premise that I have used my best endeavours to ascertain their Gaelic names, and have reason to think I have been successful in my inquiries. And here I am prompted by gratitude to acknowledge my obligations to a literary friend (well versed in the Gaelic language) who has obligingly favoured me with the etymology of the terms, or adopted names of the steps I am about to describe. These terms may be of use to the master, as they serve to distinguish the different steps from one another, and may induce a degree of speculation in the philologist. Those who have acquired a little knowledge of music, and are acquainted with Reel and Strathspey tunes, cannot but know that they are divided into two parts, each consisting of four bars, which severally contain four crotchets, or eight quavers ; and that in the generality of Strathspeys, the notes are alternately a dotted quaver and a semi-quaver, the bar frequently terminating in a crotchet.[1] This peculiar species of music is, in many parts of the Highlands, preferred to the common Reel ; on the contrary, the latter, by reason of its being the most lively tune of the two, is more generally made choice of in the dance. I have further to remark that, for the purpose of distinguishing steps, many of which do not materially differ but in their number of motions, I make use of the previous terms, *Minor, Single,* and *Double.* The first (Minor) is when it requires two steps to one bar of the tune ; the second (Single) is when one step is equal to a bar ; and the third (Double) is when it requires two bars to one step. Of the Steps.—1. *Kemshoole,*[2] or Forward Step. This is the common step for the *promenade,* or figure of the Reel. It is done by advancing the right foot forward, the left following it behind : in advancing the same foot a second time, you hop upon it, and one step is finished. You do the same motions after advancing the left foot, and so on alternately with each foot during the first measure of the tune played twice over ; but if you wish to vary the step, in repeating the measure, you may introduce a very lively one by making a smart rise, or gentle spring forward upon the right foot, placing the left foot behind it ; this you do four times, with this difference, that instead of going a fourth time behind with the left foot, you disengage it from the ground, adding a hop to the last spring. You finish the *promenade* by doing the same step, beginning with the left foot. To give the step its full effect, you should turn the body a little to the left when you go forward with the right foot, and the contrary way when you advance the left. 2. Minor *Kemkóssy,*[3] Setting or Footing Step. This is an easy familiar step, much used by the English in their country-dances. You have only to place the right foot behind the left, sink and hop upon it, then do the same with the left foot behind the right. 3. Single Kemkóssy, Setting or Footing Step. You pass the right foot behind the left to the fifth position, making a gentle bound, or spring, with the left foot, to the second position ; after passing the right foot again behind the left, you make a hop upon it, extending the left toe. You do the same step by passing the left foot twice behind the right, concluding, as before, with a hop. This step is generally done with each foot alternately, during the whole of the second measure of the tune. 4. Double Kemkóssy, Setting or Footing Step. This step differs from the single Kemkóssy only in its additional number of motions. You pass the foot four times behind the other before you hop, which must always be upon the hindmost foot. 5. Lematrást,[4] Cross Springs. These are a series of *Sissonnes.* You spring forward with the right-foot to the third or fifth position, making a hop upon the left foot, then spring backward with the right, and hop upon it. You do the same with the left foot, and so on, for two, four, or as many bars as the second part of the tune contains. This is a single step ; to double it, you do the springs forward and backward four times before you change the foot. 6. *Seby-trast,*[5] Chasing Steps, or Cross Slips. This step is like the *Balotte.* You slip the right foot before the left ; the left foot behind the right ; the right again before the left, and hop upon it. You do the same beginning with the left foot. This is a single step. 7. *Aisig-thrasd,*[6] Cross Passes. This is a favourite step in many parts of the Highlands. You spring a little to one side with the right foot, immediately passing the left foot across it ; hop and cross it again, and one step is finished ; you then spring a little to one side with the left foot, making the like passes with the right. This is a minor step ; but it is often varied by passing the foot four times alternately behind and before, observing to make a hop previous to each pass, the first excepted, which must always be a spring or bound ; by these additional motions it becomes a single step. 8. *Kem-Badenoch,* a Minor Step. You make a gentle spring to one side with the right foot, immediately placing the left behind it ; then do a single *Entrechat,* that is, a cross caper, or leap, changing the situation of the feet, by which the right foot will be behind the left. You do the same, beginning with the left foot. By adding two cross leaps to three of these steps, it becomes a double step. 9. *Fosgladh,*[7] Open Step. Slip the feet to the second position, then, with straight knees, make a smart spring upon the toes to the fifth position ; slip the feet again to the second position, and do a like spring, observing to let the foot which was before in the first spring, be behind in the second. This is a minor step, and is generally repeated during the half or the whole measure of the tune. 10. *Cuartag,*[8] Turning Step. You go to the second position with the right foot, hop upon it, and pass the left behind it ; then hop, and pass the same foot before. You repeat these alternate passes after each hop you make in going about to the right. Some go twice round, concluding the last circumvolution with two single cross capers. These circumvolutions are equal to four bars, or one measure of the tune. Others go round to the right, and then

---

[1] Here Mr. Peacock gives a note upon the resemblance of this rhythm with that of the Ossianic poetry, which we need not quote.

[2] "Or, according to its established orthography, *Ceumsiubhail,* from *Ceum,* a step, and *siubhal,* to glide, to move, to go on with rapidity."

[3] "*Ceum-coisiche,* from *Ceum,* a step, and *Coiseachadh,* to foot it, or ply the feet."

[4] "From *Leum,* a leap, a spring, and *Trasd,* across."

[5] "From *Siabadh,* to slip, and *Trasd,* across." [6] "From *Aisean,* a pass, and *Trasd,* across." [7] "An opening."

[8] "From *Cuairt,* a round, a circumvolution."

to the left. These, also, occupy the same number of bars.—Combined or Mixed Steps. These are an association of different steps, and which are necessary to add variety to the dance. For example ; you may add two of the sixth step (Soby-trast) to two of the third, (Single Kemkóssy.) This you may vary by doing the first of these steps before instead of behind ; or you may add two of the second step (Minor Kemkóssy) to one Single Kemkóssy. These steps may be transposed, so that the last shall take the place of the first. Again : two of the sixth step (Seby-trast) may be added to the fourth step (Double Kemkóssy) in going to either side. Another variety much practised is to spring backward with the right foot, instead of forward, as in the fifth step, and hop upon the left ; then spring forward, and again hop upon the same foot, and add to these two springs one Single Kemkóssy, passing the right foot behind the left. You do the same step, beginning it with the left foot. In short, without particularizing any other combinations, I shall only add that you have it in your power to change, divide, add to, or invert the different steps described, in whatever way you think best adapted to the tune, or most pleasing to yourself."—Sketch V. pages 85-98.

We have added to this Introduction some curious foreign dance-tunes, which cannot fail to be interesting to Musicians. Among these tunes are some remarkable ones of Auvergne that were promised in the Introduction to "Wood's Melodies of Scotland without Words," just published.

Peasants' Dance in the District of Bergen in Norway.

Another.

Another.

Another.

Norwegian Dance-Tune.

Norwegian Dance.

Song for Dancing; of Sarlat, in the ancient province of Perigord, now in the Department of Dordogne, in the south-west of France.

Dance-Tune of Lower Brittany.

Air of Auvergne, now in the Department of Puy-de-Dôme, Central France.

Another.

Another.

Another.

The following Dance Airs of the mountains of Auvergne were given by the Honourable George Onslow in his Violin Quartetts, op. 10.

Italian Peasants' Dance. Given by the celebrated Violinist F. M. Veracini. He visited London in 1714, and again in 1736.

In Alsace, on the Lower Rhine, there is a district named Kochersberg, the inhabitants of which differ entirely from their neighbours in manners and customs, and in their dances. The tunes of these dances have a well-marked measure of five times, and the tradition of the country assigns to them a very remote antiquity. The following is one of them, as given by A. Reicha. See his "Trente-Six Fugues."

G. F. GRAHAM.

MANUSCRIPT COLLECTIONS CONTAINING SCOTTISH MELODIES.

1 SKENE MS.—Belongs to the Library of the Faculty of Advocates. Supposed by the eminent antiquary, David Laing, Esq. of Edinburgh, to have been written about thirty or forty years after the commencement of the seventeenth century. It is written in Tablature for the Mandora, and was translated into modern musical notation by Mr. G. F. Graham, and the translation published, with a Key by Mr. Graham to the Tablature, and with a Dissertation, &c., by the late William Dauney, Esq., Advocate, in one vol. 4to, at Edinburgh, November 1838. It contains a number of Scottish airs, besides foreign dance-tunes. Mr. Laing says that the Collection was formed by John Skene of Hallyards, in Mid-Lothian, the second son of the eminent lawyer, Sir John Skene of Currichill.

2. STRALOCH MS.—Robert Gordon of Straloch's MS. Lute-book, dated 1627-29. The oldest known MS. containing Scottish airs. The original MS. is a small oblong 8vo, at one time in the library of Charles Burney, Mus. Doc.; then in that of the late James Chalmers, Esq. of London, after whose death it was sold with his other books and MSS. In January 1839, it was sent by Mr. Chalmers to Mr. David Laing of Edinburgh, for his inspection, and by Mr. Laing to Mr. G. F. Graham of Edinburgh, who had permission to copy it, and to translate and publish it. Mr. Graham made extracts from it of all the Scottish airs which it contained, and presented these extracts for preservation to the Library of the Faculty of Advocates, Edinburgh, on 26th November 1847. Some account of Robert Gordon of Straloch, who was a distinguished person in his day, will be found in the Introduction to "Wood's Songs of Scotland," vol. i. p. iv.

3 ROWALLAN MS.—A MS. Lute-book, written by Sir William Mure of Rowallan, who died in 1657, aged 63.   It
was probably written about the same time as the Straloch MS., and was a few years ago in the possession of Mr.
Lyle, Surgeon at Airth.   Its contents are chiefly foreign dance-tunes, with a very few Scottish airs.   Sir William
Mure was distinguished as a scholar and a poet.   See " Historic and descent of the house of Rowallane," from the
original MS. by Sir William, edited by the Rev. Mr. Muir, Glasgow, 1825 ; and " Ancient Ballads and Songs," by
Thomas Lyle, 1827.

4. LEYDEN MS.—Belonged to the celebrated Doctor John Leyden.   It is now in the possession of Mr. John Telfer,
Schoolmaster, Sanghtrees, Liddesdale.   It is written in Tablature for the Lyra-viol, and was sent, in 1844, to Mr.
G. F. Graham of Edinburgh, with permission to transcribe and translate from it.   The transcript which Mr.
Graham made from it, of all the tunes in Tablature, was presented to him, for preservation, to the Library of the
Faculty of Advocates, Edinburgh, on 26th November 1847.   Its date is uncertain, but cannot be earlier than
towards the close of the seventeenth century, since we find in it, " King James' March to Ireland," and " Boyne
Water," both relating to events in 1690.   It contains a number of Scottish tunes, some of which have been referred
to in the Notes to " Wood's Songs of Scotland," in 3 vols., published in 1848-49.

5. GUTHRIE (?) MS.—A number of Scottish and other tunes, in Tablature, discovered by David Laing, Esq., in a
volume of Notes of Sermons preached by James Guthrie, the Covenanting minister, who was executed in 1661, for
declining the jurisdiction of the King and Council.   See Mr. Dauney's Dissertation, pp. 139-143.   It is very
doubtful when these tunes were written, and whether they were written by the same person who penned the rest of
the volume.

6. BLAIKIE MSS.—The late Mr. Andrew Blaikie, Engraver, Paisley, was in possession of two volumes written in
Tablature, each containing a number of Scottish airs.   One of these volumes was dated 1683, and the other 1692 ;
the latter in Tablature for the *Viola da Gamba.*   The former was lost, but contained, with few exceptions, only the
same tunes as the later volume.   Both MSS. were written in the same hand.   See Mr. Dauney's Dissertation,
pp. 143-146.

7. CROCKAT MS.—This MS. Music-book is frequently referred to by Mr. Stenhouse in his Notes on Johnson's
Museum.   It is dated 1709, and belonged to a Mrs. Crockat, of whom we have not been able to learn anything
The volume was in the possession of the late Charles Kirkpatrick Sharpe, Esq.

8. MACFARLANE'S MSS.—" A Collection of Scotch Airs, with the latest Variations, written for the use of Walter
M'Farlane of that Ilk.   By David Young, W. M. [Writing Master?] in Edinburgh.   1740."   3 vols. folio.
Belongs to the Society of the Antiquaries of Scotland.   The first volume was lent many years ago, and was never
returned.

Besides these MSS. there are a few others, which are mentioned by Mr. Dauney, pp. 146, 147, of his Dissertation.
One, dating about the middle of the eighteenth century ; and another, 1706, in the possession of David Laing, Esq. of
Edinburgh ; a third, dated 1704, belonging to the Advocates' Library ; and a fourth, 1715, the property of the late Mr.
Waterston, Stationer in Edinburgh.   It is probable that several old music-books in Tablature may still be hidden in the
repositories of old Scottish families of rank ; and we would entreat the possessors of such books to rescue them from
oblivion and destruction, by sending them to some public library for preservation.   We are convinced that many such
books in Tablature have been lost or destroyed within the last two centuries, through carelessness, and from ignorance of
their value.

PRINTED COLLECTIONS OF ANCIENT AND MODERN SCOTTISH MELODIES.

1. PLAYFORD'S DANCING-MASTER.—1657.   Mr. Stenhouse, in his Notes on Johnson's Musical Museum,
refers to this work, and gives several Scottish airs from it.   Mr. Laing says, " It passed through several editions,
but the first, of 1657, is very rare, and is interesting, as perhaps the earliest printed work that exhibits several
genuine Scottish airs."   Introduction to Messrs. Blackwood's edition of Johnson's Museum, p. xxxiv.

2. D'URFEY'S COLLECTION.—1720.   Sir John Hawkins, in his History of Music, vol. iv. p. 6, says, " There
are many fine Scots airs in the Collection of Songs by the well-known Tom D'Urfey, intitled, ' Pills to purge

Melancholy,' published in the year 1720, which seem to have suffered very little by their passing through the hands of these English Masters who were concerned in the correction of that book ; but in the multiplicity of tunes in the Scots style that have been published in subsequent collections, it is very difficult to distinguish between the ancient and modern." A sixth volume appeared in 1720.

3. THOMSON'S ORPHEUS CALEDONIUS.—1725-1733. This is the earliest Collection of Scottish tunes. It contains fifty songs with the music, and also the tunes separately arranged for the flute. William Thomson was a professional Scottish musician, who went to London from Edinburgh, and attracted attention at Court by his pleasing voice and manner of singing Scottish songs, which he accompanied with the harpsichord. It would appear that W. Thomson thus brought Scottish airs into vogue in England. In 1733, a new edition of the *Orpheus Caledonius* appeared in two vols. 8vo, each containing fifty songs.

4. TEA-TABLE MISCELLANY.—About 1726. " Musick for Allan Ramsay's Collection of Scots Songs : Set by Alexander Stuart, and engraved by R. Cooper ; Vol. First. Edinburgh, printed and sold by Allan Ramsay." This very scarce volume, in five parts, is a small oblong, containing the music of seventy-one songs.

5. WATT'S MUSICAL MISCELLANY.—1729-1731 This Collection, in six vols. small 8vo, contains a number of Scottish airs and songs.

6. CRAIG'S COLLECTION.—1730. " A Collection of the choicest Scots Tunes, adapted for the Harpsichord or Spinnet," &c., by Adam Craig. Oblong folio. Craig was a violin-player and teacher of music in Edinburgh, and died in October 1741.

7. MUNRO'S COLLECTION.—1732. Alexander Munro, a Scotsman, published in Paris a Collection of twelve Scottish tunes with variations, adapted to the German Flute. The French Royal Privilege bears date 1732.

8. JAMES OSWALD'S COLLECTIONS.—1740-1742. There are three of these Collections ; the first published in Edinburgh, and the two others in London. He published also several other volumes, under the name of " The Caledonian Pocket Companion," in twelve parts. Oswald was originally à dancing-master in Dunfermline, and afterwards came to Edinburgh, where he taught dancing and music. He finally settled in London. His hoaxing of the public by ascribing certain Scottish tunes to David Rizzio, Queen Mary's Secretary, has been fully discussed in the Notes to " Wood's Songs of Scotland," *passim*.

9. WALSH'S COLLECTION.—About 1740. " A Collection of Original Scotch Songs, with a thorough-bass to each Song," &c., by J. Walsh, London. This consists of songs published on single leaves, and among them English imitations of Scottish songs.

10. WALSH'S COUNTRY-DANCES.—A Collection, in eight vols., of Scottish dance-tunes then in vogue, hut containing many that are not Scottish.

11. BARSANTI'S COLLECTION.—1742. " A Collection of Old Scots Tunes, with the Bass for Violoncello or Harpsichord," &c., by Francis Barsanti. Edinburgh. Folio, pp. 15. Barsanti was a native of Lucca, and born about 1690. He came to London in 1714, and afterwards to Edinburgh, but returned to London about 1750, where he was obliged to seek for subsistence by playing the viola in the Opera and Vauxhall Orchestras, and where he died in extreme poverty.

12. MACGIBBON'S COLLECTIONS.—1742-1755. William M'Gibbon was a Scottish violin-player of some celebrity in his day, and for many years led the Gentlemen's Concert at Edinburgh. He was a pupil of William Corbett, an Englishman, then leader of the Opera Orchestra in the Haymarket. M'Gibbon died at Edinburgh, 3d October 1756.

13. BREMNER'S COLLECTIONS.—1749-1764. Thirty Scots Songs for a Voice and Harpsichord. Edinburgh, about 1749. A second Set of Do. Edinburgh. Twelve Scots Songs for a Voice or Guitar, with a Thorough-Bass adapted for that instrument. Edinburgh, 1760. Two Collections of Scots Reels or Country-Dances, with a Bass for the Violoncello or Harpsichord. London, 1764 ? A curious Collection of Scots Tunes, with variations, for the Violin and a Bass for the Violoncello or Harpsichord. 1759. The Songs in the Gentle Shepherd, adapted to the Guitar. 1759. Thirty Scots Songs, by Robert Bremner. The words by Allan Ramsay. London. The Freemason's Songs, &c. 1759. Robert Bremner died at Kensington, 12th May 1789.

14. BURKE THUMOTH'S AIRS.—About 1760. Twelve Scotch and twelve Irish Airs, with variations, set for the German Flute, Violin, or Harpsichord, by Mr. Burke Thumoth. Vol. I. London. Royal 8vo. A second volume was published, containing the same number of airs.

15. GENERAL REID'S MINUETS, &c.,—1770. A Sett of Minuets and Marches, inscribed to the Right Hon. Lady Catharine Murray, by J[ohn] R[eid,] Esq., London; printed and sold by R. Bremner, in the Strand. Oblong 4to. General Reid published also "Six Solos for the German Flute or Violin, with a Thorough-Bass for the Harpsichord, by J[ohn] R[eid,] Esq., a Member of the Temple of Apollo. London; printed for J. Oswald." Oblong folio. "A Second Sett of Six Solos," &c. "Captain Reid's Solos." Sold also by Bremner.

16. CLARK'S FLORES MUSICÆ.—1773. "Flores Musicæ, or the Scots Musician, being a general Collection of the most celebrated Scots Tunes, Reels, Minuets, and Marches, adapted for the Violin, Hautboy, or German Flute, with a Bass for the Violoncello or Harpsichord. Published the 1st June 1773, by J. Clark, plate and seal engraver, printer, &c." Folio, pp. viii. 8vo. This contained twenty-two tunes. The work was advertised to be published in 20 numbers, but all that is now known of it consists of 32 pages containing 126 tunes, most of them with variations.

17. LORD KELLY'S MINUETS, &c.—1774. "The favourite Minuets performed at the Fête Champêtre, given by Lord Stanley at the Oaks, and Composed by the Right Honourable the Earl of Kelly. London: William Napier, Strand." The Earl of Kelly distinguished himself as a violinist and composer. He was the first Scotsman who composed overtures for an orchestra. He studied music in Germany under the elder Stamitz, and died at Brussels, 9th October 1791, in the fifty-first year of his age. Dr. Burney, in his History of Music, (vol. iv. p. 677,) says of Lord Kelly:—"He had a strength of hand on the violin, and a genius for composition, with which few professors are gifted."

18. NEIL STEWART'S COLLECTIONS.—"Thirty Scots Songs adapted for a Voice and Harpsichord. The words of Allan Ramsay. Edinburgh, Book 1st. N. Stewart and Co."—The same, Book 2d.—The same, Book 3d. "A New Collection of Scots and English Tunes, adapted to the Guitar," &c.—About 1760. "A Collection of the newest and best Minuets," &c.—About 1770. Contains some of Lord Kelly's Minuets. "A second Collection of Airs and Marches, for two Violins," &c. "A Collection of Scots Songs, adapted for a Voice and Harpsichord," &c. Folio. About 1790.

19 DOW'S MINUETS.—About 1775. "Twenty Minuets and sixteen Reels or Country-Dances, for the Violin, Harpsichord, or German Flute. Composed by Daniel Dow. Edinburgh," &c. Oblong 4to, pp. 36. "Collection of Ancient Scots Music, (Highland Airs,) by Daniel Dow." "Thirty-seven new Reels and Strathspeys for the Violin," &c. Edinburgh. About 1770. Oblong folio, pp. 44. Dow was a teacher of music in Edinburgh.

20. PEACOCK'S AIRS.—About 1776. "Fifty favourite Scotch Airs, for a Violin, German Flute, and Violoncello, with a Thorough-Bass for the Harpsichord," &c., &c., by Francis Peacock. London.

21. MACLEAN'S COLLECTION.—About 1773. "A Collection of favourite Scots Tunes, with variations for the Violin, and a Bass for the Violoncello or Harpsichord. By the late Mr. Charles M'Lean, and other eminent masters." Edinburgh: N. Stewart. Oblong folio, pp. 37.

22 M'GLASHAN'S COLLECTIONS.—About 1778. "A Collection of Strathspey Reels, with a Bass for the Violoncello or Harpsichord. By Alexander M'Glashan, Edinburgh. Printed for A. M'Glashan, and sold by Neil Stewart." Oblong folio, pp. 34. "A Collection of Scots Measures, Hornpipes, Jigs, Allemands, Cotillons, and the fashionable Country-Dances, with a Bass for the Violoncello or Harpsichord. By Alexander M'Glashan. Edinburgh: Neil Stewart." Oblong folio, pp. 36.

23. CUMMING'S COLLECTION.—1780. "A Collection of Strathspey or Old Highland Reels. By Angus Cumming, at Grantown, in Strathspey. Edinburgh, 1780." Oblong folio, pp. 20.

24. MACDONALD'S HIGHLAND AIRS.—1781. "A Collection of Highland Vocal Airs, never hitherto published. To which are added a few of the most lively Country-Dances, or Reels, of the North Highlands and Western Isles; and some specimens of Bagpipe music. By Patrick M'Donald, Minister of Kilmore in Argyleshire." Edinburgh. Folio, pp. 22 and 43.

25. NEIL GOW'S REELS.—"A Collection of Strathspey Reels, with a Bass for the Violoncello or Harpsichord. By Neil Gow, at Dunkeld. N. Stewart, Edinburgh."

26. NATHANIEL GOW'S COLLECTIONS.—1799-1824. Six different Collections of Strathspeys and Reels. Edinburgh. Folio. Three volumes of Selections from the three first Collections, with additions. Edinburgh. Folio. Four volumes of a Repository of Scots Slow Airs, Strathspeys, and Dances. Edinburgh. Folio. Two volumes of Scots Vocal Melodies. Edinburgh. Folio. A Collection of ancient curious Scots Melodies. Edinburgh. Folio. See Mr. R. Chambers's Biographical Dictionary, Neil and Nathaniel Gow.

27. JOHN AND ANDREW GOW'S COLLECTION of Slow Airs, Strathspeys, and Reels.   Folio, pp. 36.

28. AIRD'S COLLECTION.—About 1784.   A Selection of Scotch, &c., Airs, adapted to the Fife, &c.   3 vols. small oblong; each containing 200 Airs.   Glasgow.

29. JOHN RIDDELL'S COLLECTION.—A Collection of Scots Reels, Minuets, &c., &c.   Composed by John Riddell, in Ayr.   2d Edition.   Glasgow: James Aird.   Oblong 4to, pp. 60.

30. MACDONALD'S REELS.—About 1786.   A Collection of Strathspey Reels, &c.   Composed by Malcolm Macdonald.   Glasgow: J. Aird.   Oblong 4to, pp. 24.   In the third volume of Aird's Collection, Malcolm Macdonald is called "Violoncello-player to Neil Gow."

31. CORRI'S COLLECTION.—About 1788.   "A new and complete Collection of the most favourite Scots Songs," &c.   Edinburgh: Corri and Sutherland.   2 thin vols. folio.   Contains a portrait of Neil Gow.

32. NAPIER'S COLLECTIONS.—1790.   "A Selection of the most favourite Scots Songs," &c.   By William Napier.   London.   One vol. folio.   "A Selection of Original Scots Songs," &c.   Harmonized by Haydn.   London One vol. folio, 1792.   A third volume was entered at Stationers' Hall in 1794.

33. CAMPBELL'S COUNTRY-DANCES.—About 1790.   "Campbell's First Book of new and favourite Country-Dances and Strathspey Reels," &c.   Printed and sold by William Campbell.   London.   Oblong 4to.   Twelve Books.

34. BRYSON'S COLLECTION.—1791.   "A curious Collection of favourite Tunes," &c.   J. Bryson, High Street, Edinburgh.

35. THE MUSICAL MISCELLANY.—1792.   "The Edinburgh Musical Miscellany," &c.   Selected by D. Sime.   Edinburgh: W. Gordon.   One vol. 12mo.   A second volume, printed for John Elder, Edinburgh, 1793.

36. GEORGE THOMSON'S COLLECTIONS.—1793, &c.   A particular list of these, furnished by Mr. Thomson himself, will be found in the Introduction to the first volume of "Wood's Songs of Scotland," 1848.   Mr. G. Thomson's Collections are now, by purchase, the property of Messrs. Wood and Co., Edinburgh.

37. MACKINTOSH'S REELS, &c.—1793.   "Sixty-eight new Reels, Strathspeys, and Quick Steps," &c.   Composed by Robert Mackintosh.   Printed for the Author.

38. DALE'S COLLECTION.—1794.   A Collection of Scottish Songs, in 3 Books.

39. RIDDELL'S COLLECTION.—1794.   "A Collection of Scotch, Galwegian, and Border Tunes," &c.   Selected by Robert Riddell of Glenriddell, Esq.   Edinburgh: Johnson and Co.   Folio, pp. 37.   "New Music for the Pianoforte or Harpsichord," &c., consisting of Reels, Minuets, &c.   [By Robert Riddell, Esq.]   Edinburgh: James Johnson.   Folio.

40. RITSON'S COLLECTION.—1794.   Scottish Songs, in two vols. 12mo.   London.

41. URBANI'S COLLECTION.—About 1794.   "A Selection of Scots Songs," &c.   By Peter Urbani.   Edinburgh and London.   Three vols. folio, 1794-97-99.

42. THE VOCAL MAGAZINE.—1797-98-99.   Royal 8vo.   Edinburgh: C. Stewart & Co.

43. ROSS'S COLLECTION.—"A Select Collection of ancient and modern Scottish Airs," for the voice, with accompaniments, &c.   By John Ross, Organist, St. Paul's, Aberdeen.   Edinburgh: John Hamilton.   Folio, pp. 62.

44. WHYTE'S COLLECTION.—"A Collection of Scottish Airs," &c.   Harmonized, &c., by Joseph Haydn, Mus. Doc.   Published at Edinburgh by William Whyte.   Two vols. folio.   1806.

45. JOHN ELOUIS' SELECTION of Scots Songs.   Two vols. folio.   1806-7.

46. ARCHIBALD DUFF'S (ABERDEEN) SELECTION of Airs, &c., with Reels, Strathspey, and Country Dances.   Folio, pp. 50.   1812.

47. CAPTAIN SIMON FRASER'S COLLECTION of Highland Airs.   Folio.   Edinburgh, 1816.

48. ALEXANDER CAMPBELL'S ALBYN'S ANTHOLOGY.—Two vols. folio.   Edinburgh, 1816 and 1818.

49. WALKER AND ANDERSON'S MINIATURE MUSEUM of Scots Songs and Music.   1818.   2 vols. 12mo.   Edinburgh.

50. MARSHALL'S COLLECTION.—One vol. folio. Edinburgh: Alexander Robertson. 1822.

51. R. A. SMITH'S SCOTTISH MINSTREL. Six vols. 8vo. R. Purdie, Edinburgh. The 6th vol. dated 1824.

52. POPULAR NATIONAL MELODIES.—Adapted for the Pianoforte. By James Dewar. Six Numbers, folio. Alexander Robertson, Edinburgh. About 1826.

53. DAVIE'S CALEDONIAN REPOSITORY of the most favourite Scottish Slow Airs, Marches, Strathspeys, Reels, Jigs, Hornpipes, &c., &c. Expressly adapted for the Violin. In four Books, oblong 8vo. Wood and Co., Edinburgh. 1829.

54. D. M'KERCHER'S (DUNKELD) COLLECTIONS (3) of Strathspeys and Reels. Edinburgh, 1830, et seq. Folio.

55. THE VOCAL GEMS OF SCOTLAND.—Arranged with new and appropriate Symphonies and Accompaniments for the Pianoforte. By J. M. Müller. In two vols. folio. Wood and Co., Edinburgh. 1837-1839.

56. DUN AND THOMSON'S COLLECTION.—New edition of the Vocal Melodies of Scotland, arranged with Symphonies and Accompaniments for the Pianoforte. By Finlay Dun and John Thomson. Published by Paterson and Roy, Edinburgh. This Collection consists of four vols. folio, each containing thirty-six songs. First vol. published in 1837.

57. JOHNSON'S SCOTS MUSICAL MUSEUM.—New Edition, with notes. Six vols. 8vo. Blackwoods, Edinburgh, 1839.

58. JAMES DANIEL'S COLLECTION of Airs, Strathspey Reels, &c. Aberdeen, 1840. Folio, pp. 39.

59. THE DANCE MUSIC OF SCOTLAND.—A Collection of all the best Reels and Strathspeys, both of the Highlands and Lowlands, arranged for the Pianoforte. By J. T. Surenne. In one volume, folio. Wood and Co., Edinburgh, 1841.

60. THE GARLAND OF SCOTIA, &c.—The Airs are for Voice, Flute, or Violin. One vol. 8vo. Glasgow : William Mitchison. 1841.

61. WILSON'S SONGS OF SCOTLAND.—Eight Books, folio. 1842.

62. VOCAL MELODIES OF SCOTLAND.—Arranged for the Pianoforte, with an Accompaniment for the Flute and Violoncello, (ad libitum.) By Alfred Devaux. Six Books, folio. London: Cramer and Co. Edinburgh. Paterson and Roy. 1842.

63. GEMS OF SCOTTISH MELODY.—With new and appropriate Symphonies and Accompaniments for the Pianoforte. Edited by W. Montignani. One vol. 4to. T. and W. M'Dowall, Edinburgh. 1844.

64. LOWE'S COLLECTION of Reels, Strathspeys, and Jigs, being a new and complete Selection of the best Dancing Tunes in their proper keys, carefully arranged with appropriate basses for the Pianoforte and Violoncello. In six Books, folio. Paterson and Roy, and Wood and Co., Edinburgh. 1844-45.

65. WOOD'S SONGS OF SCOTLAND.—Edited by G. F. Graham. Three vols. royal 8vo. Edinburgh : Wood and Co 1848-49.

66. ORAIN NA'H ALBAIN.—A Collection of Gaelic Songs with English and Gaelic words, and an Appendix containing traditional notes to many of the Songs. The Pianoforte accompaniment arranged and revised by Finlay Dun. One vol. folio. Wood and Co., Edinburgh, &c., &c. 1848.

67. HAMILTON'S SELECT SONGS OF SCOTLAND.—Folio. Glasgow, 1848.

68. LAYS FROM STRATHEARN.—By Caroline, Baroness Nairne, &c., arranged, &c., for the Pianoforte by Finlay Dun. One vol. folio. London: Addison and Co. Edinburgh: Paterson and Roy, and J. Purdie. 1850.

69. NAPIER'S SELECTION of Dances and Strathspeys. London. Folio, pp. 36.

70. JOHN HAMILTON'S COLLECTION of Strathspeys and Reels. Edinburgh. Oblong 4to. Caledonian Museum. Three books. Edinburgh.

71. JOHN M'INTYRE'S COLLECTION.—Edinburgh. Folio, pp. 40.

72. DONALD GRANT'S COLLECTION.—Edinburgh. Folio, pp. 38.

73. ISAAC COOPER OF BANFF'S COLLECTION.

74. T. H. BUTLER'S SELECT COLLECTION of Scottish Airs with Accompaniments. Edinburgh: Muir, Wood, and Co.

75. GEORGE JENKINS' COLLECTION of Scottish Slow Airs and Dance Music. Folio, pp. 70.

76. JOHN CLARK'S (OF PERTH) COLLECTION of Strathspey Reels and Country-Dances. Folio, pp. 21.

77. JAMES WALKER'S (OF DYSART) COLLECTIONS (2) of Reels, Strathspeys, Jigs, &c. Folio.

78. JOHN GUNN'S THIRTY FAVOURITE SCOTCH AIRS, for Violin, Flute, or Violoncello. Folio. London.

79. DOMENICO AND NATALE CORRI'S SELECT COLLECTION of forty Scots Songs, with Accompaniments, &c.; 4th Edition. Edinburgh.

80. JOSHUA CAMPBELL'S COLLECTION of New Reels and Strathspeys. Glasgow. Folio, pp. 48. Collection of Favourite Tunes with Variations, for Violin, &c. Glasgow. Royal 8vo, pp. 81.

81. JOHN ALEXANDER MAY'S SELECTION of Songs, &c., for German Flutes. Glasgow. Oblong royal 8vo. pp. 120.

82. J. M'FADYEN'S REPOSITORY of Scots and Irish Airs, Strathspeys, &c., for two Violins and Bass. Oblong royal 8vo, pp. 128.

83. CHARLES DUFF'S (DUNDEE) COLLECTION of Strathspey Reels, &c. Folio, pp. 36.

84. ABRAM MACINTOSH'S Thirty new Strathspey Reels, &c. Edinburgh. Folio, pp. 11.

85. ALEXANDER LEBURN'S (AUCHTERMUCHTY) COLLECTION of Strathspey Reels, &c. Edinburgh. Folio, pp. 12.

86. WILLIAM CHRISTIE'S (CUMENSTOWN) COLLECTION of Strathspey Reels, &c. Edinburgh. Folio, pp. 40.

87. DANIEL ROBERTSON'S COLLECTION of Reels, Strathspeys, &c. Edinburgh. Folio, pp. 26.

88. ALEXANDER MACKAY'S (ISLAY) COLLECTION of Reels, Strathspeys, &c. Glasgow. Folio, pp. 36.

89. WILLIAM MORRISON'S COLLECTION of Strathspeys, Reels, &c. Inverness. Folio, pp. 36.

90. ROBERT PETRIE'S (AT KIRKMICHAEL) COLLECTIONS (4) of Strathspey Reels, &c. Edinburgh and London. Folio.

91. MALCOLM M'DONALD'S (DUNKELD) COLLECTIONS (4) of Strathspey Reels, &c. Folio. Edinburgh.

92. JOHN BOWIE'S (PERTH) COLLECTION of Strathspey Reels, &c. Edinburgh. Folio, pp. 35.

93. WILLIAM SHEPHERD'S COLLECTION of Strathspey Reels, &c. Edinburgh. Folio, pp. 26.

94. ROBERT MACKINTOSH'S COLLECTIONS (4) of Airs, Reels, Strathspeys, &c. Edinburgh and London. Folio.

95. JOHN MORRISON'S (OF PETERHEAD) COLLECTION of Strathspeys and Reels. Folio, pp. 23.

96. JAMES PORTEOUS' COLLECTION of Reels and Strathspeys. Edinburgh. Folio, pp. 40.

97. THE CALEDONIAN MUSEUM, &c., for the Flageolet, Flute, or Violin. Three Books, oblong 4to. Edinburgh: Alexander Robertson.

NOTE.—To Mr. A. J. Wighton of Dundee, who possesses an extensive collection of printed Scottish Music, we are indebted for the titles of some of the works contained in the above List.   G. F. G

INDEX

TO

THE DANCE MUSIC OF SCOTLAND.

b

THE DANCE MUSIC OF SCOTLAND.

NOTE.

It will be observed that the tunes are in general arranged in sets of three, a Reel, Strathspey, and Reel, this being the succession in which they are usually performed. A chord has been added at the end of those sets where the last tune does not finish in the key; this is of course to be played once only, at the close of the dance.

As there are but two distinct movements throughout the work, the Editor has deemed it unnecessary to affix the Metronome mark to each tune.

The movement of the Reel is $\bigtriangledown$ = 126 Maelzel.

that of the Strathspey is $\bigtriangledown$ = 94 Maelzel.

The only exception to this is the Reel of Thulican, or Tulloch, the time of which is $\bigtriangledown$ = 120.

THE DUCHESS OF ROXBURGHE.

REEL.

LENNOX LOVE TO BLANTYRE.

REEL.

THE COUNTESS OF LOUDON.

STRATHSPEY.

CLYDESIDE LASSES.

REEL.

RATHA FAIR.

REEL.

BRECHIN CASTLE.

STRATHSPEY.

LADY MONTGOMERY.

REEL.

COLONEL M'BAIN.

REEL.

TULLOCHGORUM.

STRATHSPEY.

MERRY LADS OF AYR.

REEL.

SIR DAVID HUNTER BLAIR.

REEL.

MONYMUSK.

STRATHSPEY.

CHARLIE STUART.

REEL.

THE HIGH ROAD TO LINTON.

REEL.

THE MARQUIS OF HUNTLY.

HIGHLAND FLING.

STRATHSPEY.

MRS. MACLEOD OF RASAY.

REEL.

D. C.

LORD DALHOUSIE.

REEL.

THE BRAES O' TULLYMET.

STRATHSPEY.

THE GATHERING.

REEL.

THE ISLE OF SKYE.

REEL.

LADY SHAFTESBURY.

STRATHSPEY.

MISS GIBSON.

REEL.

CAPTAIN KENNEDY.

MASTER FRANCIS SITWELL.

THE DRUMMER.

REEL.

THE FIFE HUNT.

REEL.

MRS. GARDEN OF TROUP.

STRATHSPEY.

THE COUNTESS OF SUTHERLAND.

REEL.

JOHNNIE'S FRIENDS ARE NE'ER PLEASED.

REEL.

NIEL GOW.

STRATHSPEY.

SALLY KELLY.

REEL.

THE MASON'S APRON.

REEL.

THE DUCHESS OF GORDON.

STRATHSPEY.

THE BACK OF THE CHANGE-HOUSE.

REEL.

LOCH EARN.

THE AYRSHIRE LASSES.

THE DUKE OF PERTH.

REEL.

NEW CHRISTMAS.

REEL.

LADY MARY RAMSAY.

STRATHSPEY.

JENNY DANG THE WEAVER.

REEL.

THE DEIL AMANG THE TAILORS.

REEL.

MISS DRUMMOND OF PERTH.

STRATHSPEY.

MISS FLORA M'DONALD.

REEL.

TORRY BURN.

REEL.

LADY CHARLOTTE CAMPBELL.

STRATHSPEY.

FIGHT ABOUT THE FIRESIDE.

REEL.

LADY HARRIET HOPE.

REEL.

THE ROYAL RECOVERY.

STRATHSPEY.

FAIR FA' THE MINSTREL.

MART DO CHRO 'A MHEINANICH.

REEL.

C

LADY MADELINA SINCLAIR'S BIRTH-DAY.

REEL.

NEIL GOW'S WIFE.

STRATHSPEY.

JOHN CHEAP THE CHAPMAN.

REEL.

DUILLATER HOUSE.

BROWN'S REEL.

REEL.

THE MARQUIS OF HUNTLY.

STRATHSPEY.

THE HIGHLANDMAN.

REEL.

AMULREE.

REEL.

THE DUKE OF GORDON'S BIRTH-DAY.

STRATHSPEY.

LADY MARY STOPFORD.

REEL.

THE DUKE OF ROXBURGHE.

REEL.

LADY MADELINA SINCLAIR.

STRATHSPEY.

THE WIND THAT SHAKES THE BARLEY.

REEL.

CAPTAIN KEELER.

REEL.

LADY BINNING.

STRATHSPEY.

THE M'FARLANE RANT.

REEL.

THE PARKS OF FOCHABERS.

REEL.

DONALD DOW.

STRATHSPEY.

LADY DUMFRIES.

REEL.

THE DIAMOND.

REEL.

THE HONOURABLE CAPTAIN MAITLAND.

STRATHSPEY.

THE REEL OF BOGIE.

REEL.

THE BOATMAN OF PITNACREE.

REEL.

THE MARQUIS OF HUNTLY'S FAREWELL.

STRATHSPEY.

MISS DUMBRECK.

REEL.

FILL THE STOUP.

REEL.

THE MILLER OF DRONE.

STRATHSPEY.

THE BRIDGE OF PERTH.

REEL.

THE LASS OF BALLANTRAE.

REEL.

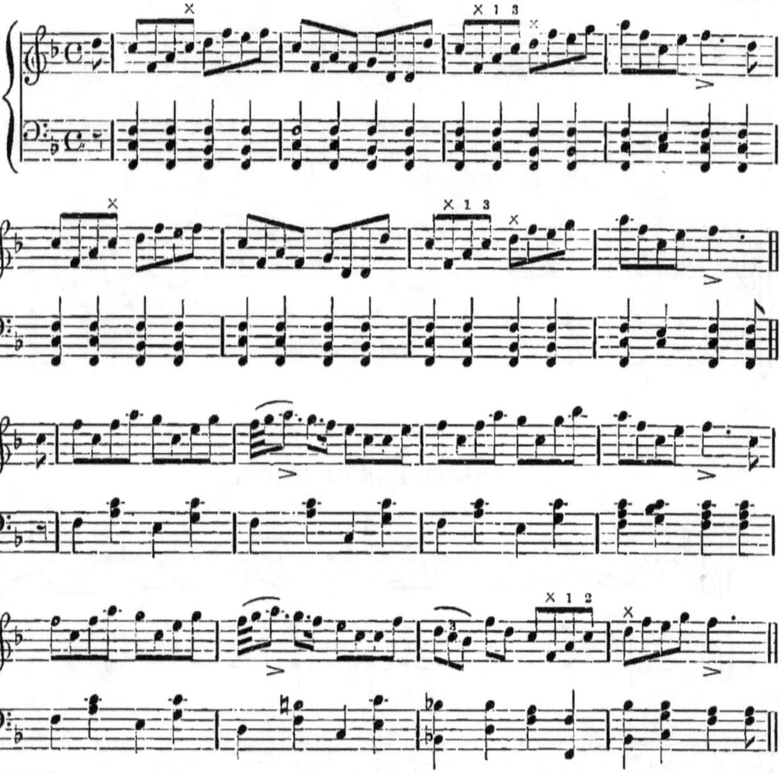

LADY DOUNE.

STRATHSPEY.

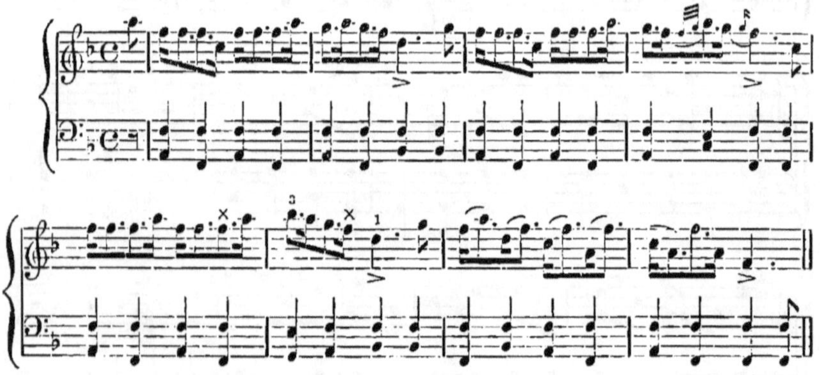

MISS HOPKINS.

REEL.

MISS JESSIE STEWART.

REEL.

MRS. ADYE.

STRATHSPEY.

MISS WHITEFORD.

BEEL.

GIORNOVICHI.

REEL.

LORD RAMSAY.

STRATHSPEY.

I'LL GANG NAE MAIR TO YON TOUN.

REEL.

THRO' THE WOOD SHE RAN.

REEL.

LADY ELIZABETH LINDSAY.

STRATHSPEY.

THE RETICULE.

REEL.

THE STEWARTS' RANT.

REEL.

THE DUCHESS OF GORDON.

STRATHSPEY.

CAPTAIN MACDUFF.

REEL.

THE PERTHSHIRE HUNT.

REEL.

STRUAN ROBERTSON'S RANT.

STRATHSPEY.

SLEEPY MAGGIE.

REEL.

THRO' THE WOOD OF FAVIE.

REEL.

LADY LUCY RAMSAY.

STRATHSPEY.

MISS JOHNSTON.

REEL.

D. C. fz.

JOHN STEWART.

REEL.

WILLIE WINKIE.

STRATHSPEY.

EARL MARISCHAL.

REEL.

LADY BETTY BOYLE.

THE DUCHESS OF ATHOLE.

DUCHESS' SLIPPER.

STRATHSPEY.

ATHOLE HOUSE.

REEL.

THE BRIDGE OF BRACKLIN.

REEL.

THE NORTH BRIDGE OF EDINBURGH.

STRATHSPEY.

THE ARGYLE BOWLING-GREEN.

REEL.

THE OLD MAN.

REEL.

BEN LOMOND.

STRATHSPEY.

THE BRIDGE OF TURK.

REEL.

THE AULD STEWARTS BACK AGAIN.

LADY ANN STEWART.

THE FYKET.

REEL.

MISS WEDDERBURN.

REEL.

DALRY HOUSE.

STRATHSPEY.

O BUT YE BE MERRY.

O SHE'S COMICAL.   REEL.

MISS CHARLOTTE STEWART.

REEL.

SANDERS BRANE.

STRATHSPEY.

THE CAMERONIAN RANT.

REEL.

THE MARQUIS OF BEAUMONT.

REEL.

LORD SEAFORTH.

STRATHSPEY.

CAWDOR FAIR.

REEL.

KINCALDRUM.

REEL.

MISS HOPE.

STRATHSPEY.

DALKEITH HOUSE.

REEL.

LORD MACDONALD.

REEL.

LADY CHARLOTTE CAMPBELL.

STRATHSPEY.

LADY CHARLOTTE CAMPBELL.

REEL.

MRS. COMPTON OF CARHAM-HALL.

REEL.

BEN NEVIS.

STRATHSPEY.

PRETTY PEGG.

REEL.

SANDY O'ER THE LEA.

REEL.

STUMPIE.

STRATHSPEY.

THE FOX CHASE.

REEL.

THE REEL OF THULICHAN.

COUTIE'S WEDDING.

TAYMOUTH CASTLE.

REEL.

MRS. RACHEL GIBSON.

REEL.

CAPTAIN PRINGLE OF YAIR.

STRATHSPEY.

MISS CHARLOTTE ROSS.

REEL.

MISS NISBET OF DIRLETON.

REEL.

GENERAL WEMYSS.

STRATHSPEY.

JOCKEY LATIN.

REEL.

MISS MAULE OF PANMURE.

REEL.

HILTON LODGE.

STRATHSPEY.

DELVIN HOUSE.

REEL.

CAPTAIN BYNG.

REEL.

COILANTOGLE.

STRATHSPEY.

DUNSE DINGS A'.

REEL.

MISS FORBES.

REEL.

SIR ALEXANDER DON.

STRATHSPEY.

LAMBERTON RACES.

REEL.

MISS BAIRD OF SAUGHTON HALL.

REEL.

DAINTIE DAVIE.

STRATHSPEY.

LADY MARY DUNDAS.

LADY GRACE DOUGLAS.

REEL.

LORD DOUNE.

STRATHSPEY.

THE HONOURABLE MISS CHARTERIS.

REEL.

LADY MARGARET STEWART.

REEL.

DELVIN SIDE.

STRATHSPEY.

THE EARL OF BREADALBANE'S HERMITAGE.

REEL.

THE COUNTESS OF HADDINGTON.

MISS HAMILTON OF BANGOWR.

DUNROBIN CASTLE.

REEL.

MISS ANN STEWART.

REEL.

NIEL GOW'S RECOVERY.

STRATHSPEY.

THE HIGHLAND SKIP.

REEL.

THE FISHER'S WEDDING.

REEL.

THE HAUGHS OF CROMDALE.

STRATHSPEY.

THE GLASGOW LASSES.

REEL.

BONNIE ANNIE.

REEL.

MISS GRIEVE OF HOWDAN.

STRATHSPEY.

THE MARQUIS OF TULLYBARDINE.

REEL.

LORD MACDONALD.

O MITHER, ONY BODIE BUT THE DUDDY BLACKSMITH. (OLD SET.) REEL.

LORD ALEXANDER GORDON.

STRATHSPEY.

PEASE STRAE.

REEL.

FLOORS CASTLE.

REEL.

MARRY KETTY.

STRATHSPEY.

MISS DOUGLAS.

REEL.

MISS RAMSAY.

REEL.

THE DUCHESS OF HAMILTON.

STRATHSPEY.

THE PIRRIWIG.

AN FHIR'CHRUAIG.   REEL.

MARY GRAY.

REEL.

CAMERON'S WIFE.

STRATHSPEY.

MRS. SCOTT MONCRIEFF.

REEL.

LADY SUSAN HARRIET KER.

CALLAM SHIARGHLAS.

STRATHSPEY.

MISS RITCHIE.

THE WHIGS OF FIFE.

REEL.

THE YETTS OF MUCKART.

STRATHSPEY.

BRODIE HOUSE.

REEL.

THE CIRCUS.

REEL.

MRS. ROBERTSON OF ALEXANDRIA.

STRATHSPEY.

MISS MARY ANNE ROBERTSON.

SIR RONALD M'DONALD.

REEL.

JOHN ROY STEWART

STRATHSPEY.

THE EARL OF EGLINTON.

REEL.

THE NINE PINT COGGIE.

REEL.

DON SIDE.

STRATHSPEY.

AS A THOISEACH.

KEEP IT UP.

REEL.

OSSIAN'S HALL.

REEL.

MRS. MORAY OF ABERCAIRNEY.

STRATHSPEY.

THE COUNTESS OF ELGIN.

REEL.

JOHNNIE MADE A WEDDING O'T.

REEL.

CORIMONIE'S RANT.

STRATHSPEY.

SIR GEORGE MACKENZIE OF COUL.

REEL.

THE MULLIN DHU.

PANMURE HOUSE.

GILLIE CALLUM.

REEL.

MRS. WILSON.

REEL.

THE EARL OF LOUDON.

STRATHSPEY.

BORLUM'S RANT.

REEL.

THE BANKS OF SPEY.

REEL.

LADY BAIRD.

STRATHSPEY.

RORY MACNAB.

REEL.

THE KEEL ROW.

REEL.

THE KIRN.

HARVEST HOME.   STRATHSPEY.

RACHEL RAE.

REEL.

LORD KELLY.

REEL.

MR. MORAY OF ABERCAIRNEY.

STRATHSPEY.

MISS JANE STEWART.

REEL.

MR. MENZIES OF CULDARES.

REEL.

HIGHLAND WHISKY.

STRATHSPEY.

MISS STEWART OF GARTH.

REEL.

THE EARL OF DALKEITH.

REEL.

MRS. BAIRD OF NEWBYTH.

STRATHSPEY.

MISS GEORGINA SCOTT.

REEL.

THE MERRY LADS OF FOSS.

REEL.

MR. ROBERTSON OF LUDE.

STRATHSPEY.

CUTTYMUN AN' TREELADLE.

MRS. M'DONALD OF CLANRANALD.

REEL.

LADY MACKENZIE OF COUL.

STRATHSPEY.

MRS. DRUMMOND OF LOGIEALMOND.

REEL.

THE HONOURABLE COLONEL WEMYSS.

REEL.

THE DUCHESS OF MANCHESTER.

STRATHSPEY.

THE BRAES OF MARR.

REEL.

MISS ROSE OF TARLOGIE.

REEL.

MONRO'S RANT.

STRATHSPEY.

BLACK BUT COMELY.

REEL.

THE BOBERS O' BRECHIN.

REEL.

LADY GWYDYR.

STRATHSPEY.

GLEN LYON.

REEL.

MRS. ALEXANDER BRODIE.

REEL.

LIEUTENANT-COLONEL BAILLIE OF LEYS.

STRATHSPEY.

CAIRNGORM.

CHEAP MEAL.   REEL.

THE MARQUIS OF HASTINGS.

LORD MOIRA.

STRATHSPEY.

Edinburgh University Press
THOMAS AND ARCHIBALD CONSTABLE, PRINTERS TO HER MAJESTY.

www.ingramcontent.com/pod-product-compliance
Lightning Source LLC
Chambersburg PA
CBHW020536270326
41927CB00006B/597